I AM....

(Positive Affirmations For Children)

By Ayesha Rodriguez

 This book
is for

_____

From

_____

Library of Congress Cataloging-in-Publication Data
ISBN: 978-1-7356650-5-4

Publisher Jaye Squared Youth Empowerment Services, INC.
Website: www.ayesharodriguez.com

Illustration copyright © 2016 by Rina Risnawati

Layout Design by Susan Gulash
Gulash Graphics, Lutz, FL

This book is dedicated to you. I hope you enjoy it!
You are incredible, just the way you are!

TABLE OF CONTENTS

I was born to do great things, some big and some small.

I am here to make a difference and spread love to all.

I am special.

I have a roof over my head and food on the table.

I am happy for a family who provides what they are able.

I am thankful.

I talk about my problems when I am feeling down.

There are people who care about me and want to turn my frown upside down!

I am loved.

I eat healthy foods like fruits and veggies.

I make sure to run, play and do my stretches.

I am healthy.

I treat all people the way I want to be treated.

It is important to be nice and help others when it is needed.

I am kind.

There is so much to learn when I am in school.

So I make sure to practice my reading, math, and science too!

I am smart.

We are all different and come in many colors and sizes.

The only thing that matters is what is inside of us.

I am important.

I love my body and the person that I am.

I will be the best that I can be and give it all that I can.

I am happy.

I am special.
I am thankful.
I am loved.
I am healthy.
I am kind.
I am smart.
I am important.
I am happy.

I am glad to be me!

Daily Activity:

Stand in the mirror every day and repeat all of the sentences that start with the words I am. I want you to really believe it, just like I do! If people say things to you that are not nice, you will know in your heart that it is not true!

You are amazing and I'm
so proud of you.

Discussion Questions:

1. How do you think the boy in the wheelchair feels to have children playing with him?
2. What does it mean to have "special needs"?
3. What are some things that your family provides for you?
4. What are you thankful for?
5. Who do you talk to when you are feeling sad?
6. What healthy foods do you like to eat?
7. What exercises do you enjoy?
8. When was the last time you helped someone? How did it make you feel?
9. What do you love about yourself?
10. Name some things that you would like to get better at. What will you do to improve?
11. Why is it important to study?
12. The only thing that matters is what is inside of us. What does that mean to you?

Are there more affirmations that you would like to add? Write them in pencil below.

1. I am_____

2. I am_____

3. I am_____

4. I am_____

5. I am_____

6. I am_____

7. I am_____

8. I am_____

About the Author

Ayesha Rodriguez is the president of a 501c3 children's nonprofit organization, entrepreneur, author, speaker and most importantly, a mother of two. She is very passionate about education and making a positive impact in the community.

Made in the USA
Monee, IL
17 September 2020